Test Your Professional English

Hotel and Catering

Alison Pohl

Series Editor: Nick Brieger

PENGUIN ENGLISH

Pearson Education Limited
Edinburgh Gate
Harlow
Essex CM20 2JE, England
and Associated Companies throughout the world.

978-0-582-45161-2

First published under the title *Test Your Business English: Hotel and Catering* 1996
This edition published 2002
Text copyright © Alison Pohl, 1996, 2002
Eighth impression 2011

Designed and typeset by Pantek Arts Ltd, Maidstone, Kent
Test Your format devised by Peter Watcyn-Jones
Illustrations by David Eaton and Vince Silcock
Printed in China.   SWTC/08

Acknowledgements
I am indebted to Nick Brieger for many things, but as far as this book is concerned, for
help, support and encouragement. Tim Harrison and Bernard Houssin were very
generous with their time and expertise and I am truly grateful for their comments and
suggestions. My thanks are also extended to Helen Parker and everyone at Penguin
Longman Publishing.

Alison Pohl

Published by Pearson Education Limited in association with Penguin Books Ltd, both
companies being subsidiaries of Pearson plc.

For a complete list of the titles available from Penguin English please visit our
website at www.penguinenglish.com, or write to your local Pearson Education office
or to: Marketing Department, Pearson Education Ltd, Edinburgh Gate, Harlow,
Essex CM20 2JE.

Contents

Section 7 Management

Section 8 Financial affairs

To the student

Do you use English in your work or in your studies? Perhaps you are a student of hotel and catering. Perhaps you are working in a hotel or catering establishment in an English speaking country or need English to communicate with customers and colleagues from other countries. Whatever your background, the tests in this book will help you improve your professional English. You can check your knowledge of key vocabulary and essential expressions and see how they work in context, so that you can communicate more effectively and confidently in your work or in your studies.

The book has been divided into eight sections. Each section deals with an important topic area in the hotel and catering industry including hotel services, food service and management. You may choose to work through the book from beginning to end or may find it more useful to select tests according to your interests and needs.

Many tests also have tips (advice) on language, language learning and professional information. Do read these explanations and tips: they are there to help you.

To make the book more challenging and more fun, many different kinds of tests are used, including sentence transformation, gap-filling, word families, multiple choice and crosswords. There is a key at the back of the book so that you can check your answers; and a word list to help you revise key vocabulary.

Vocabulary is an important part of language learning and this book will help you to develop your specialist vocabulary. When you are learning vocabulary, notice how words are used (grammar) and when they are used (context). Perhaps you only need to recognise certain items of vocabulary when you read or hear them but if you need to be able to use them yourself at a later date, practise making sentences of your own. The tests in this book will help you check what you know and increase your knowledge of new concepts and terms in a structured and systematic way.

Alison Pohl

The full series consists of:

Test Your Professional English: Accounting	Alison Pohl
Test Your Professional English: Business General	Steve Flinders
Test Your Professional English: Business Intermediate	Steve Flinders
Test Your Professional English: Finance	Simon Sweeney
Test Your Professional English: Hotel and Catering	Alison Pohl
Test Your Professional English: Law	Nick Brieger
Test Your Professional English: Management	Simon Sweeney
Test Your Professional English: Marketing	Simon Sweeney
Test Your Professional English: Medical	Alison Pohl
Test Your Professional English: Secretarial	Alison Pohl

1 Name the place

Use the clues to fill in the missing letters in these words.

1	The passage between several rooms.	c o r r i d o r
2	Guests can buy newspapers and magazines here.	k _ _ _ _
3	Here you can sit outside your bedroom in the sun.	b _ _ _ _ _ _
4	Bedding and clothes are cleaned here.	l _ _ _ _ _ _
5	The entrance hall.	l _ _ _ _
6	Guests can enjoy a long drink here.	c _ _ _ _ _ _ _ b _ _
7	Guests can leave suitcases here.	l _ _ _ l _ _ _ _ _ _
8	A cool, dark room where the wine is kept!	c _ _ _ _ _
9	Here guests can eat and drink outside.	t _ _ _ _ _ _
10	Guests can sit comfortably and relax here.	l _ _ _ _ _
11	Climbing these to the top floor is tiring.	s _ _ _ _ _
12	A quick way to reach the top floor.	l _ _ _
13	Guests can hang their coats here.	c _ _ _ _ _ _ _ _
14	Food is cooked here.	k _ _ _ _ _ _
15	The place for a wedding reception.	b _ _ _ _ _ _ _ _ _ r _ _ _

The **ground floor** in the UK is called the **first floor** in the US. A **lift** in the UK is called an **elevator** in the US.

2 Helping guests 1

What does the receptionist say to the hotel guests? Write the letter of each phrase in the box next to the appropriate drawing. The first one has been done as an example.

a   Good evening, madam. May I help you?

b   Could you spell that, please?

c   I'm afraid your room isn't quite ready yet. Would you mind taking a seat in the lounge for a few minutes?

d   Sorry to keep you waiting, sir. How can I help you?

e   I'm terribly sorry that you're not happy with your room.

f   Could I possibly ask you to park your car round the back?

g   Can I suggest you try our evening entertainment? It's always very popular.

h   I'm so glad you've enjoyed your stay with us. We look forward to welcoming you again in the future.

Could you and *Could I ask you to* are followed by the base form of the verb. For example, *Could you **help** me? Could I ask you to **open** the window?* Try to make some more sentences of your own. **See also:** Test 40 How to be polite.

3 Helping guests 2

Look at the guests' requests and write the letter of the appropriate reply in the speech bubble. The first one has been done as an example.

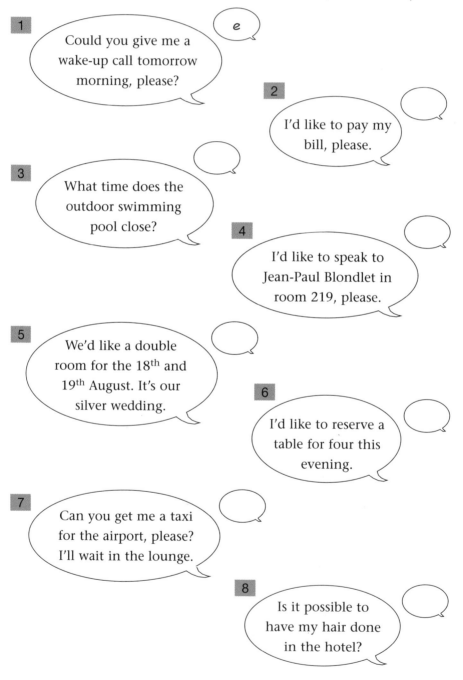

1 **e** Could you give me a wake-up call tomorrow morning, please?

2 I'd like to pay my bill, please.

3 What time does the outdoor swimming pool close?

4 I'd like to speak to Jean-Paul Blondlet in room 219, please.

5 We'd like a double room for the 18th and 19th August. It's our silver wedding.

6 I'd like to reserve a table for four this evening.

7 Can you get me a taxi for the airport, please? I'll wait in the lounge.

8 Is it possible to have my hair done in the hotel?

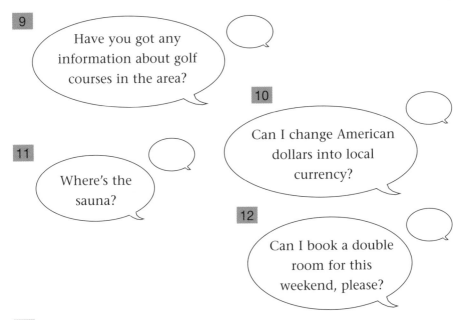

9 Have you got any information about golf courses in the area?

10 Can I change American dollars into local currency?

11 Where's the sauna?

12 Can I book a double room for this weekend, please?

a	Certainly, madam. What time would you like to eat?
b	I'm sorry, but there's no answer. Can I take a message?
c	I'm afraid we're fully booked this weekend, sir.
d	It's in the basement. Take the lift and then turn left.
e	Certainly, madam. What time would you like us to call you?
f	There's a leaflet in the stand. The best one is twenty kilometres away.
g	Usually before dark. Tonight it'll be at 7 o'clock.
h	Of course, madam. There's a hairdresser's beside the exercise room.
i	Yes, sir. You can do that at the bank. It's just opposite the hotel.
j	Certainly, madam. For such a celebration, we'll make sure you get the best room in the hotel!
k	Of course, sir. I'll call you when it comes.
l	One moment please, madam. I'll work out the total.

A **silver wedding** is the 25th wedding anniversary. Other important wedding anniversaries are the 40th (**ruby**), 50th (**golden**) and 60th (**diamond**).

4 Reception

Choose the word which best completes each sentence. The first one has been done as an example.

1 Guests entering the hotel will find the reception desk in the
_____ *foyer* _____ .

a) scullery   b) foyer

c) back office   d) corridor

---

2 One of the jobs of a receptionist is to _____ complaints.

a) manage   b) deal with

c) organize   d) regret

---

3 People who often use the same hotel are called _____ .

a) normals   b) returners

c) regulars   d) usuals

---

4 Customers with valuable items should use the _____ provision.

a) safe deposit   b) secure

c) savings   d) lock-up

---

5 The customers of a particular hotel are known as the
_____ .

a) guest list   b) long stays

c) clientele   d) usuals

---

6 When guests arrive the receptionist usually asks them to sign the
_____ .

a) register   b) bookings form

c) ledger   d) guest bill

7 Each day the _____ list shows the names of the guests expected.

a) stop-go
b) records
c) arrivals
d) room

8 If guests lose their room keys, a member of staff can open their room door with a _____ key.

a) main
b) passage
c) pass
d) card

9 Messages for guests who are out should be placed in the appropriate _____ at reception.

a) pigeon-hole
b) keyhole
c) bird box
d) key hook

10 Hotels may manage to fill vacant rooms with _____ bookings.

a) opportunity
b) chance
c) early
d) provisional

11 People who have booked but don't arrive are known as

_____ .

a) delays
b) no comers
c) failures
d) no shows

12 In order to be successful, a hotel must try to maximize room

_____ .

a) availability
b) turnover
c) status
d) occupancy

Foyer is another word for **lobby**.
See also: Test 1 Name the place.

5 At work in the front office

The word in capitals at the end of each sentence can be used to form a word that fits suitably in the blank space. The first one has been done as an example.

1 Customers can make a phone call, send a fax or e-mail or use the Internet to make a _reservation_ . RESERVE

2 We will have to make _____ for the guests' luggage to be taken straight to the airport. ARRANGE

3 We've received a booking for a party of 35 people. Could you please send them _____ ? CONFIRM

4 The receptionist will deal with all our customers' _____ . REQUIRE

5 I'm sorry, but there is no _____ for the honeymoon suite for the period you require. AVAILABLE

6 Our aim is to provide customer _____ . SATISFY

7 The customer has been taken ill, so we've had a _____ of the booking. CANCEL

8 We try very hard to meet our guests' _____ . EXPECT

9 Specific room _____ is normally done once the guests have arrived. ALLOCATE

10 One of the first jobs to be done each day is to deal with the _____ . CORRESPOND

11 When filling in the reservations form, please make sure
all the _____ are completed correctly. ENTER

12 I'm very sorry but we're fully booked tonight.
We've got no _____ at all, I'm afraid. VACANT

13 For your _____ this evening we have
organised a local jazz group, who will be
playing in the Tudor room. ENTERTAIN

14 The group organiser has just telephoned to
express his _____ for the service we
provided last week. APPRECIATE

The receptionist will deal with our customers' _____ .

Some nouns end in **-tion**, **-ment**, **-ance**, **-ence**. Can you think of some
other nouns which end in these suffixes? **See also:** Test 43 Security
measures, for more word-building exercises.

6 Reservations

The following extracts are from two different letters. One is a letter making a reservation, the other is a letter of confirmation. Put the extracts in the right order to produce two correct letters.

1	Letter of reservation

e					

2	Letter of confirmation

a Yours faithfully
Susan Peacock
Secretary

b I look forward to receiving your confirmation.

c I would like to reserve four single rooms from 19th to 24th November for four of our managers.

d We look forward to receiving our guests.

e Dear Sir/Madam

f Thank you for your letter of 16th September. We are very pleased that you have chosen to use our hotel for your four managers who will be in Perth from 19th to 24th November.

g The rooms should be booked in the names of Bill Franks, Mary Black, Erik Petersson and Ann Jones.

h Could you please inform me of your rates and whether you offer discounts for company bookings.

i I would like to confirm your reservation for four single rooms for these dates. We are happy to be able to offer you our corporate rates, details of which are enclosed.

j Yours sincerely
Peter Black
Reservations Clerk

k Dear Ms Peacock

> If a letter begins with *Dear Sir/Madam* it should end with **Yours faithfully**. You end a letter with **Yours sincerely** when the person is named in the greeting, e.g. *Dear Ms Schwartz*. A less formal way to end a letter or e-mail is **Best wishes**.

7 Checking out

Complete the sentences with one of these verbs. Use each verb once only.

calculate	~~check out~~	dispute	incur	issue	itemize	liaise
	overcharge	return	settle	sign for	vacate	

1. At the end of their stay, guests _check out_ at reception.

2. During their stay at a hotel, guests will _____ charges for the services which they use in the hotel.

3. When a hotel guest eats in the hotel restaurant, she will be asked to _____ the meal before leaving.

4. Some hotels _____ a luggage pass to show that payment has been received and the guest is free to leave.

5. The hotel should _____ the bill so that guests can see the cost of each item.

6. Most hotels ask guests who are leaving to _____ their rooms before lunchtime.

7. The computer will automatically _____ any discount.

8. The receptionist will ask the guests to _____ their bills before leaving the hotel.

9. The receptionist will _____ any valuables which have been deposited for safe keeping.

10. Guests may _____ a charge if they disagree with it.

11. Good teamwork means that the receptionist will _____ with the other departments in the hotel.

12. The hotel must be careful not to _____ the guests; they will be very unhappy if they have to pay more than they should.

8 Payment

Use the clues to fill in the missing letters in the two-word nouns below. There is one three-word noun!

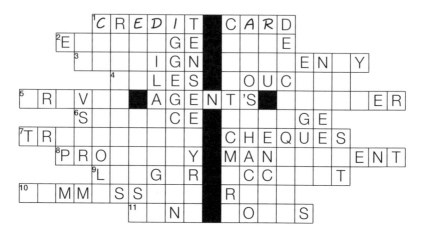

1	For example, Barclaycard, Visa or Access.
2	The number of euros to American dollars varies because of this.
3	Notes and coins from another country.
4	You sign this when you pay by 1 above.
5	Tourists who book through an agent will use this as a form of payment.
6	Often 10% or 15% added to the restaurant bill.
7	These cheques are often used by overseas customers.
8	This computer system is used for reservations, guest billing and controlling activities in the hotel.
9	Customers who regularly use the hotel may pay this monthly.
10	The level of administrative charges for changing money made by the hotel or bank.
11	Paper money.

These compound nouns above are written as two words but some compound nouns are written with a hyphen, e.g. *dining-room*; or as one word, e.g. *guidebook*. There are no rules, but a good dictionary will help you.

9 Lost property

These items have been left behind by customers. Write the letter of each item next to the correct word or words.

1	binoculars	_a_
2	cap	____
3	carrier bag	____
4	hairbrush	____
5	doll	____
6	glasses	____
7	glove	____
8	car keys	____
9	lipstick	____
10	pocket diary	____
11	purse	____
12	mobile phone	____
13	tie	____
14	toilet bag	____
15	umbrella	____

10 Hotel facilities

The following guests have different wishes. Which section of the room information sheet should they look at? Write the number of each guest next to the appropriate section. The first one has been done as an example.

1 Elaine Lu would like to have her blouse cleaned.

2 Ben Krozac wants to know about buses to the airport.

3 The Nakatas would like breakfast in their room.

4 Ms Lewis is feeling unwell.

5 Mr Dixon needs clean shoes for the morning.

6 Jutta Koch would like a massage and manicure.

7 Mrs Peterson has to be sure she gets up early tomorrow morning.

8 Marie Frelimo wants to call her friend in Barcelona.

9 Tom Moshi would like a soft drink in his room.

10 Yana Valk wants to know where to leave her car.

11 Eric and Thomas wonder what they can do this evening.

12 Edward Chung wants to know the prices for different rooms.

INFORMATION

Room service	____	Tariffs	____
Telephone	____	Entertainment	____
Minibar	____	Shoe-cleaning service	____
Transport	____	Wake-up calls	____
Laundry	_1_	Garaging	____
Medical help	____	Hairdressing and Beauty	____

11 Hotel accommodation

A Match the plan on the left with its definition on the right.

American plan   bed only

Demi-pension   bed and breakfast

European plan   bed, breakfast and lunch or dinner

Continental plan   bed, breakfast, lunch and dinner

B Write the name of each room type below the correct picture.

adjoining
double
double en suite
single
~~twin~~

a

_____twin_____

b

c

d

e

_____   _____

Notice the difference between a **twin** and a **double** room. It's a good idea
to check with guests whether they want a double bed or two single beds.

12 Out and about

Complete the sentences with one of these words. Use each word once only. There are more words than you need. Read the whole text first before trying to fill the gaps.

attractions	conveniences	countryside	courtesy	cruise	daily
destination	displayed	~~escorted~~	events	excursions	ferries
festivals	galleries	guides	itinerary	locality	museums
nature	resort	ruins	scenery	souvenirs	

Visitors arriving at the hotel will be interested to know what is on offer. Many hotels will arrange (1) _____escorted_____ tours by coach, or on foot, to visit a variety of local (2) _____ . These may include the crumbling (3) _____ of historic buildings, art (4) _____ to see paintings and sculptures or (5) _____ , where objects from the past are displayed.

Many people prefer to spend time out of doors and like to travel into the (6) _____ , where they can enjoy and photograph the (7) _____ . The hotel can arrange half-day or full-day (8) _____ and a detailed (9) _____ will inform the guests of the exact route which will be taken. Guests are normally given some time to visit and buy (10) _____ to remind them of their holiday when they get home. Alternatively, they may enjoy a boat (11) _____ on a river or canal.

During the year there are many (12) _____ taking place in the local area. Information about the time and place of these should be (13) _____ in the hotel so that guests are aware of what is going on. The hotel can expect to be very busy when national or local (14) _____ are taking place. Some of these are famous all over the world and attract many visitors.

13 Giving directions

Complete the missing words in the sentences. There are several possibilities for some of them. The first one has been done as an example.

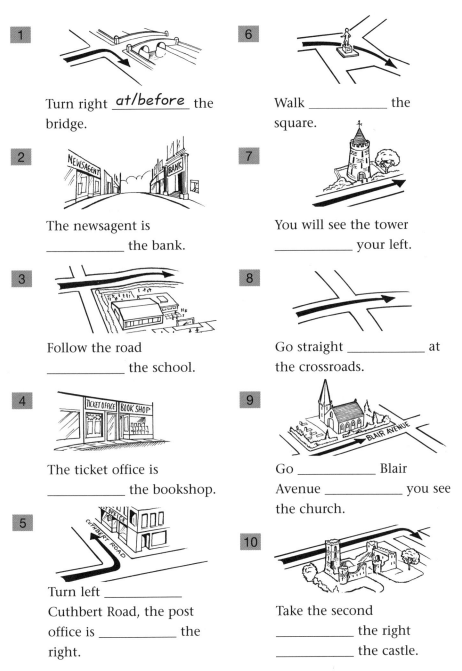

1. Turn right _at/before_ the bridge.

2. The newsagent is _____ the bank.

3. Follow the road _____ the school.

4. The ticket office is _____ the bookshop.

5. Turn left _____ Cuthbert Road, the post office is _____ the right.

6. Walk _____ the square.

7. You will see the tower _____ your left.

8. Go straight _____ at the crossroads.

9. Go _____ Blair Avenue _____ you see the church.

10. Take the second _____ the right _____ the castle.

14 Conferences 1

Fill in the crossword. Some letters have been added to help you.

Across

3 Connected to your computer this will project images. (10, 9)

7 This can be fixed to the wall and used for writing on.

8 These are quick to move and need less room for storage. (7, 6)

10 A video can be viewed on this.

12 Conferences will require different room layouts. A room set out with chairs only is called _____ style.

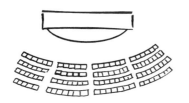

13 In a large room or hall speakers may need one of these so that they can be heard at the back!

Down

1 A room layout where chairs and tables are provided is referred to as _____ style.

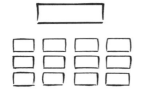

2 Seats which are easy and quick to move. (8, 6)

4 Organizers will probably require this equipment to show diagrams and text on the wall. (8, 9)

5 The visitors will need these regularly throughout the day!

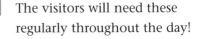

6 This will welcome the visitors and give them information about where their meeting is taking place.

9

10

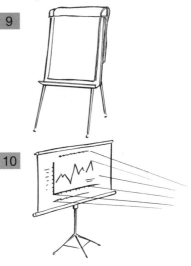

15 Conferences 2

Complete the sentences with one of these words. Use each phrase once only.

> annual   conference package   duration   estimated attendance
> finalize   function sheet   postpone   provisional   ~~venue~~

Planning the conference

The place where the conference is held is known as the

(1) _____venue_____ . The expected number of guests is known as the

(2) _____ . To begin with the dates will probably only be

(3) _____ , but closer to the time of the conference they will

have to be confirmed. The conference (4) _____ may be two,

three or several days. If it's held once a year, it's known as an

(5) _____ event. A conference hotel will probably calculate

all the costs of the conference and offer the customer one total price

called the (6) _____ . The hotel will list all the conference

requirements in the (7) _____ . A few days before the

conference begins, the hotel should (8) _____ all the

arrangements with the conference organizers. If there's a problem, it

may be necessary to (9) _____ the conference to a later date.

> Event management computer software is used in many hotels for bookings,
> costing and billing. Some also include a module for the allocation of
> equipment.

conference programme   delegates   hospitality room
opening ceremonies   plenary   seating capacity   speakers
square metres   syndicate

Practical matters

The people who come to the conference are known as the
(10) _____ , while the people who are invited to give a talk
at a conference are known as the (11) _____ . When
describing the size of a room, the maximum number of people who can
sit in the room is known as the (12) _____ . The size of
rooms is given in (13) _____ . When all the participants are
present for one session, a large (14) _____ room will be
required. Smaller (15) _____ rooms for small groups of two
to ten people may be needed too. Guests are welcomed in the
(16) _____ . The (17) _____ shows the guests
what is happening where and when. A conference begins with the
(18) _____ .

When all the participants are present for one session,
a large _____ room will be required.

16 The correct reply

Some guests are experiencing problems. Write the letter of the appropriate reply in the speech bubble. The first one has been done as an example.

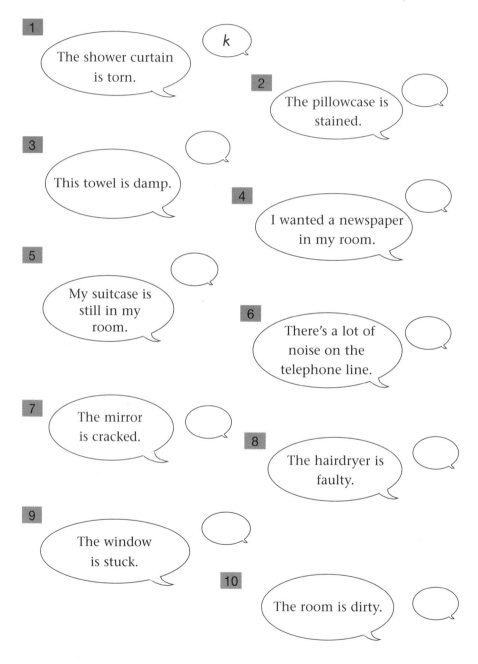

1

The shower curtain is torn.

k

2

The pillowcase is stained.

3

This towel is damp.

4

I wanted a newspaper in my room.

5

My suitcase is still in my room.

6

There's a lot of noise on the telephone line.

7

The mirror is cracked.

8

The hairdryer is faulty.

9

The window is stuck.

10

The room is dirty.

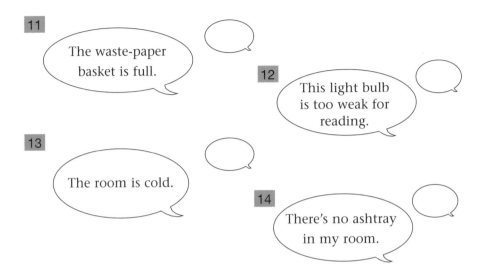

11 The waste-paper basket is full.

12 This light bulb is too weak for reading.

13 The room is cold.

14 There's no ashtray in my room.

a I'll get the chambermaid to clean it.

b I'll have the heating turned up.

c I'll get someone to open it.

d I'll have it brought down.

e I'll fetch you a dry one.

f If you tell me which one you read, I'll have it delivered.

g I'll get you a clean one.

h I'll have it replaced.

i I'll have a stronger one fitted.

j I'll have one brought to your room.

k I'll have a new one put up.

l I'll have it checked.

m I'll call the operator and have it checked.

n I'll get someone to empty it.

I will is always used in the reduced form, i.e. *I'll*, to offer help. *I will* often sounds rude when offering assistance.

17 Handling customer complaints

Complete the telephone dialogue with these expressions. Use each expression once only.

> assure   at our expense   bringing this incident   can you tell me
> could you   deeply regret   how can I   I must apologise
> if you would accept   I'm sorry to   I'm terribly sorry
> ~~may I ask~~   of course   one moment   right

Customer: I'd like to speak to the restaurant manager. What's his name?

Receptionist: Of course, madam. Our restaurant manager is a lady, Magda Illich. (1) ___May I ask___ your name?

Customer: It's Mrs Peacock of Peacock Enterprises.

Receptionist: (2) _____ , Mrs Peacock and I'll ask Magda Illich to speak to you.

Manager: Good afternoon Mrs Peacock. (3) _____ help?

Customer: I have a complaint to make about the service I received here yesterday.

Manager: (4) _____ what the problem was?

Customer: I was entertaining business clients and your waiter managed to seat one of my guests at the wrong table.

Manager: (5) _____ hear that, madam.

Customer: I haven't finished. The same waiter managed to spill a few drops of wine on another guest's jacket and then, instead of apologising, he said it was only a few drops and we shouldn't get so upset!

Manager: (6) _____ about this Mrs Peacock.
(7) _____ tell me which table you were
sitting at?

Customer: It was the large round table by the window.

Manager: (8) _____ for the waiter's remarks and I
(9) _____ you I will speak to him.

Customer: But what are you going to do about my client's jacket?

Manager: We will (10) _____ pay for the jacket to be
dry-cleaned. I (11) _____ the
embarrassment you have been caused and ask
(12) _____ a voucher for four people
to have a meal here (13) _____ .

Customer: That sounds reasonable.

Manager: Thank you for (14) _____ to our attention.
This is the only way we can put problems
(15) _____ .

'It's only a few drops ...'

It costs five times as much to attract a new customer as it does to keep an
existing one! So remember: listen, sympathise, apologise, offer compensation
and thank the customer for bringing the problem to your attention.

18 The building

Choose the word which best completes each sentence.

1 The restaurant is closed for two months while it is being
_____renovated_____ .

  a) renewed   b) remade

  c) renovated   d) reformed

---

2 There will be ten new bedrooms when the builders finish the

_____ .

  a) extension   b) extent

  c) enlargement   d) utility

---

3 The chalets have everything a guest could require: they are

_____ .

  a) self-catered   b) self-formed

  c) self-made   d) self-contained

---

4 The building has fallen into a state of _____ and now
needs a lot of work.

  a) despair   b) dispersal

  c) disrepair   d) distress

---

5 This room is very quiet as it's not at the front of the hotel. It is

_____ .

  a) back-looking   b) rear-facing

  c) rear-looking   d) back-facing

---

6 The building is very old and the management have spent a lot of
money _____ the original features.

  a) restoring   b) installing

  c) re-equipping   d) servicing

7 We apologize for any inconvenience caused during the
_____ of the new swimming pool.
a) composition   b) formation
c) assembly   d) construction

8 The new restaurant is to be built on the _____ of the
old factory which was pulled down three years ago.
a) site   b) position
c) ground   d) basis

9 The present location of the restaurant is not good and now Mr
Martin is looking for new _____ .
a) places   b) premises
c) estates   d) resorts

10 The _____ around the hotel are beautifully planted
with flowers.
a) earth   b) floors
c) grounds   d) land

The building has fallen into a state of _____ .

19 Furniture and fittings

Write the letter of each item next to the correct word or words.

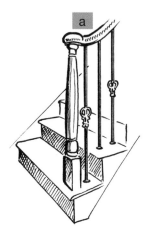

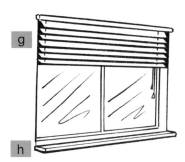

1	banister	*a*
2	bedside cabinet	___
3	bedspread	___
4	blind	___
5	bookcase	___
6	ceiling	___
7	coat-hanger	___
8	coat-stand	___
9	curtains	___
10	curtain rail	___
11	desk	___
12	door handle	___

13	duvet	_____
14	hairdryer	_____
15	light switch	_____
16	luggage rack	_____
17	minibar	_____
18	picture frame	_____
19	pillow	_____
20	sheet	_____
21	skirting	_____
22	tie-back	_____
23	wardrobe	_____
24	windowsill	_____

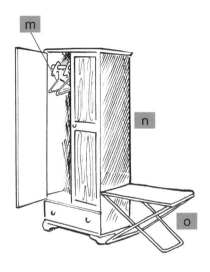

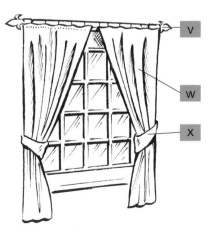

20 The bathroom

Write the letter of each item next to the correct word or words.

1	bath	_d_	7	mirror	____	13	soap	____
2	bath mat	____	8	pedal bin	____	14	tap	____
3	bath towel	____	9	plug	____	15	toilet	____
4	glass	____	10	shower	____	16	toilet paper	____
5	hand towel	____	11	shower cap	____	17	washbasin	____
6	light switch	____	12	shower curtain	____			

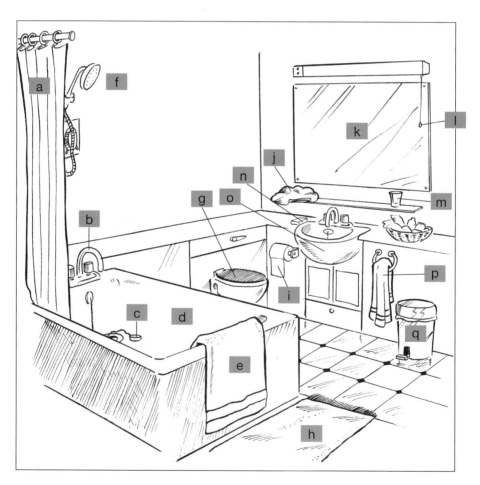

21 Cleaning 1

Complete the sentences with one of these verbs. Use each verb once only.

damp wipe	deep clean	dispose	dry-clean	launder	polish
replenish	rinse	scrub	soak	strip	~~sweep~~	vacuum	wet mop

1   *Sweep*   the floor with the brush to remove all the dust and grit.

2   _____ the furniture and floors to make them shine.

3   _____ the floor with a brush, water and disinfectant.

4   _____ the floor with water, disinfectant and cloths.

5   _____ the shelves and the furniture with a wet cloth so you don't spread the dust.

6   _____ the bedlinen by washing and drying.

7   _____ cloths in clean water to remove the soap after washing.

8   _____ the white bedlinen in solution for a few hours to make it easier to remove stains.

9   _____ the bedding because you can't wash it in water.

10   _____ the carpets, chairs and sofas to remove the dust.

11   _____ the beds once the guests have left and take the linen to the laundry.

12   _____ the soap, shampoo and shower gel each morning.

13   _____ of all the waste safely so that no infection occurs.

14   _____ the carpets thoroughly with chemical solution.

22 Cleaning 2

Rearrange the letters to form the correct words.

1   If silver isn't cleaned it will ____*tarnish*____ .   RASHITN

2   Don't touch the glass window or you will
leave _____ .   FINPITSGRERN

3   Be careful if there is water on the floor as
it will be _____ .   ERSLYPPI

4   Children having a bath often _____ .   SHLASP

5   Nasty smells in a room are known as _____ .   RSOOUD

6   Don't use _____ cleaning agents
because they will scratch the surface.   RASABEVI

7   Machines which make work quicker and
easier are known as _____ devices.   LOUBAR - AVNGSI

8   In some regions the water is hard and leaves
_____ on baths.   EMILSLECA

9   Sometimes white cotton becomes yellow or grey
and you can use _____ to whiten it again.   BLCHAE

10   If red wine is spilt on the carpet, it will
leave a _____ .   NSITA

11   Some waste, e.g. paper and empty cans, can be
sold and, therefore, has a _____ value.   SALGEAV

12   Old pieces of metal may leave brown _____
marks on fabrics.   STUR

13   _____ are used to remove marks which
will not come out in water.   ENTSSVOL

14   There will only be light _____ on carpets
which are not often used.   SOAGEIL

15   A special leather which is used for cleaning
windows is called a _____ .   AMCHIOS

23 Hotel systems 1

Complete the sentences with one of these words. Use each word once only.

> drains   extractor   filters   grill   humidity   insulated   pipes
> radiator   sewer   tank   thermostat   U-bend   ~~ventilation~~

Air

In large building complexes, fresh air will be supplied to rooms through an air-conditioning system. This provides (1) __*ventilation*__ in each room so that guests can breathe comfortably. It also controls the (2) _____ so that the air doesn't contain too much moisture. In each room the opening to the air-conditioning system is covered with a (3) _____ .

In kitchens, steam and smells are sucked out by an (4) _____ , which also contains (5) _____ to remove any harmful gases.

Central heating

Heating may be underfloor or a (6) _____ may be fitted to the wall in each room. The temperature in the room can be controlled by means of a (7) _____ , which will maintain a constant temperature. An efficient system will be well (8) _____ so that energy is not lost.

Water

Water required for a building may be stored in a (9) _____ .
Water is supplied to each room through (10) _____ . Waste water is removed through (11) _____ which enter a main (12) _____ outside the building.

Under baths and basins a (13) _____ stops smells entering the room.

24 Hotel systems 2

Complete the sentences with one of these words. Use each word once only.

~~appliances~~	current	electrician	flex	fuse	kilowatt hours
	overloaded	plug	socket	wiring	

Electricity

A hairdryer or an electric shaver are examples of electrical

(1) _appliances_ . They have a (2) _____ with a

(3) _____ at the end which fits into a (4) _____ in

the wall. If there is a fault, the electricity supply will be cut off by

a (5) _____ .

The amount of electricity used is measured in (6) _____ .

The electrical (7) _____ in Britain is 240 volts, while in many

European countries it is 220 volts. If too many pieces of equipment

are connected to one supply, the system may be (8) _____

and there is a danger of fire. When problems arise, a qualified

(9) _____ should be called to check the (10) _____ .

In most countries there is legislation to cover the use of electrical
appliances as well as **wiring** systems. In the UK it is not permitted to have
electric **sockets** or **switches** in a bathroom other than bathroom shaver
sockets. Lights must have a cord pull or be switched on/off outside the
bathroom.

25 Fruit

Write the letter of each fruit next to the correct word or words.

1 avocado   _b_

2 blackcurrants ____

3 cherries   ____

4 grapefruit   ____

5 grapes   ____

6 kiwi fruit   ____

7 mango   ____

8 melon   ____

9 passion fruit ____

10 pawpaw   ____

11 peach   ____

12 pineapple   ____

13 plums   ____

14 star fruit   ____

15 strawberry   ____

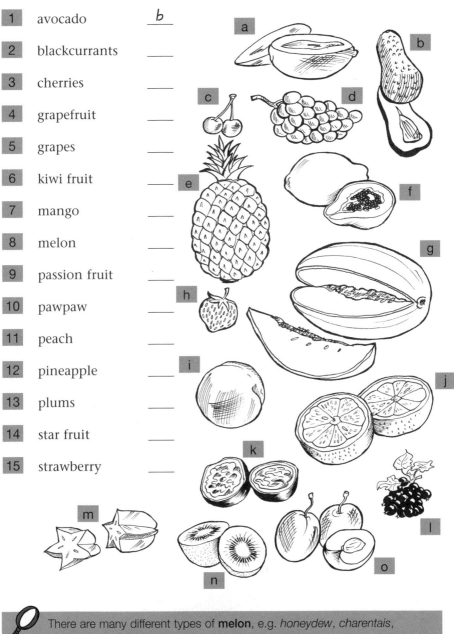

There are many different types of **melon**, e.g. *honeydew*, *charentais*, *cantaloupe*, *ogen* and of course *watermelon*. They are different in colour, size and texture.

26 Vegetables

Write the letter of each vegetable next to the correct word or words.

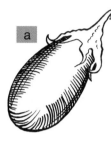

1	artichoke	_k_
2	asparagus	___
3	aubergine	___
4	butter-beans	___
5	cabbage	___
6	cauliflower	___
7	courgette	___
8	cucumber	___
9	French beans	___
10	lettuce	___

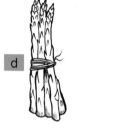

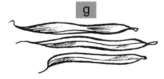

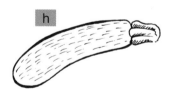

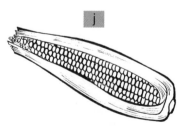

11	mushrooms	——
12	okra	——
13	onion	——
14	peas	——
15	pepper	——
16	pumpkin	——
17	radish	——
18	sweetcorn	——
19	tomato	——

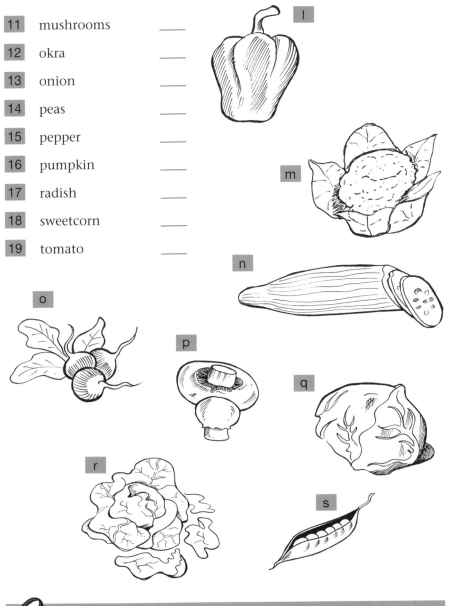

- Because of air transport, it is possible to get most vegetables all year round. Despite this, many vegetables such as **pumpkin** and **asparagus** have generally remained seasonal.

- **Courgettes** are sometimes known as **zucchini**, **aubergine** is known as **eggplant** and **French beans** are often simply referred to as **green beans**.

27 Classifications

Write the name of each group. The first one has been done as an example.

1	milk, cream, butter, yogurt	_dairy products_
2	almond, Brazil, pistachio, cashew	n _ _ _
3	haricot beans, lentils, chickpeas, soya beans	p _ _ _ _ _
4	coriander, parsley, thyme, basil	h _ _ _ _
5	ginger, cinnamon, cloves, turmeric	s _ _ _ _ _
6	pork, lamb, beef, mutton	m _ _ _
7	sultanas, currants, raisins, prunes	d _ _ _ _ f _ _ _ _
8	choux, flaky, puff, short	p a _ _ _ _
9	royal, glacé, satin, butter	i _ _ _ _
10	spaghetti, tagliatelle, ravioli, lasagne	p _ _ _ _
11	cod, seabass, trout, salmon	f _ _ _
12	tea, coffee, orange juice, cola	b _ _ _ _ _ _ _ _
13	claret, Rioja, Chianti, Sekt	w _ _ _
14	pheasant, grouse, venison, rabbit	g _ _ _
15	consommé, fish, broth, chowder	s _ _ _ _
16	Gouda, Stilton, Camembert, Parmesan	c _ _ _ _ _ _
17	mussels, oysters, scallops, prawns	s _ _ _ _ _ _
18	fruit, gateau, sponge, Swiss roll	c _ _ _ _
19	hollandaise, béchamel, mornay, Bearnaise	s _ _ _ _ _
20	wheat, rye, oats, barley	c e _ _ _ _ _

28 Taste

Complete the sentences with one of these adjectives. Use each adjective once only.

> bitter bland burnt delicious dry greasy hot rancid rich
> salty savoury sour spicy stale sweet tender

1   The skin of an orange tastes quite ____bitter____ .

2   Food cooked with chilli is _____ .

3   Food cooked with a lot of cream is very _____ .

4   Sugar and honey will make a dish _____ .

5   Indian food is _____ .

6   If you forget the salt and pepper, the food will be _____ .

7   Lemon juice is _____ .

8   Food cooked with salt and spices is _____ .

9   Too much fat used in cooking can make the food _____ .

10   A dish without enough liquid is _____ .

11   A dish cooked to perfection will be _____ .

12   Toast cooked for too long tastes _____ .

13   Snack foods such as crisps and peanuts are often very

_____ .

14   High-quality meat which is easy to cut is _____ .

15   Bread and cakes delivered four days ago will be _____ .

16   Butter or fat left in the sun will melt and go _____ .

29 Preserving food

Rearrange the letters to form the correct words.

1. ___Smoking___ preserves the food and also adds some lovely flavours. It is used for fish and meat. **KINSMGO**

2. _____ seals the foods in airtight tins which are heated at a high temperature to kill any harmful organisms. **ANCNING**

3. _____ removes the moisture from food to stop bacteria and moulds growing. It can be used for vegetables, herbs, fruit and fish. **YNGIDR**

4. The use of _____ is allowed by law to help preserve food, but the manufacturers must tell you which have been used. **CHELICAMS**

5. _____ removes the air from around the food so it keeps longer. **CAVUMU-INGPAKC**

6. _____ involves putting carbon dioxide, nitrogen or carbon dioxide around the food to stop bacteria and moulds growing. **ASG STAGEOR**

7. _____ keeps the food at low temperatures so that microorganisms don't increase in numbers in the food. **INGFRZEE**

8. _____ is a traditional way of preserving fish and meat, preventing the growth of microorganisms. **INGLTSA**

9. _____ involves exposing foods to energy waves which kill bacteria. This is not allowed in every country. **RATONDIAI**

10. _____ , using high concentrations, prevents moulds and bacteria from growing. Jams are a good example. **SUARGING**

Food will spoil if it is not preserved because of micro-organisms called **moulds**, **yeasts** and **bacteria** which exist in the air. Fruit ripens because of **enzymes** in the fruit. These same enzymes also cause fruit to over-ripen and spoil.

30 Cooking

Replace the words in **bold type** with a single word from the list a–n.

1 **Cook** the bread **in dry heat in the oven** for about fifty
minutes.   _f_

2 To keep meat moist when roasting, **cover** it **regularly
with melted fat.**   ____

3 **Decorate** the vegetables with some parsley.   ____

4 Let the soup **cook slowly, just below boiling point.**   ____

5 The meat is **cut into tiny pieces in a machine** for this recipe. ____

6 One method of cooking fish is to **cook it in lots of very hot fat.** ____

7 Could you **remove the skin and bones from** the fish, please? ____

8 When the potatoes are cooked, **crush** them **to a pulp.**   ____

9 **Remove the outside skin** of the potatoes.   ____

10 Guests may like eggs which have been **broken into boiling
water and vinegar.**   ____

11 Make sure the frozen chicken has completely **thawed** before
cooking.   ____

12 **Cut** the carrot **into small squares.**   ____

13 **Add salt and pepper** before serving the soup.   ____

14 You can **improve the taste of** the sauce with vanilla.   ____

a	dice	h	flavour
b	minced	i	defrosted
c	deep fry	j	mash
d	season	k	peel
e	poached	l	fillet
f	bake	m	simmer
g	garnish	n	baste

31 Utensils

Write the letter of each utensil next to the correct word or words.

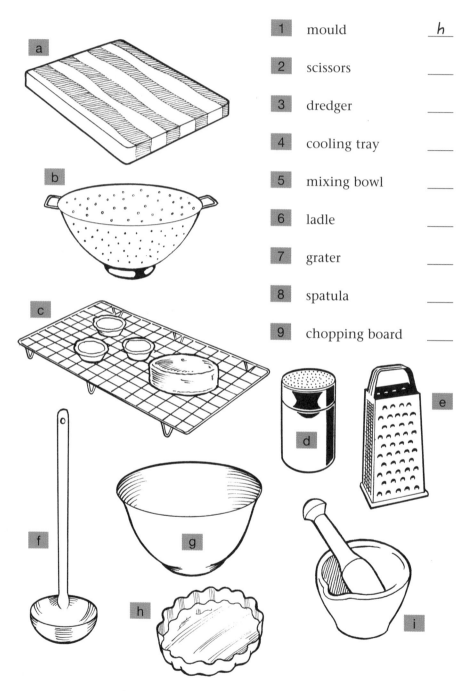

1	mould	*h*
2	scissors	___
3	dredger	___
4	cooling tray	___
5	mixing bowl	___
6	ladle	___
7	grater	___
8	spatula	___
9	chopping board	___

10 peeler ___

11 rolling pin ___

12 mortar and pestle

___

13 skimmer ___

14 whisk ___

15 colander ___

16 steel ___

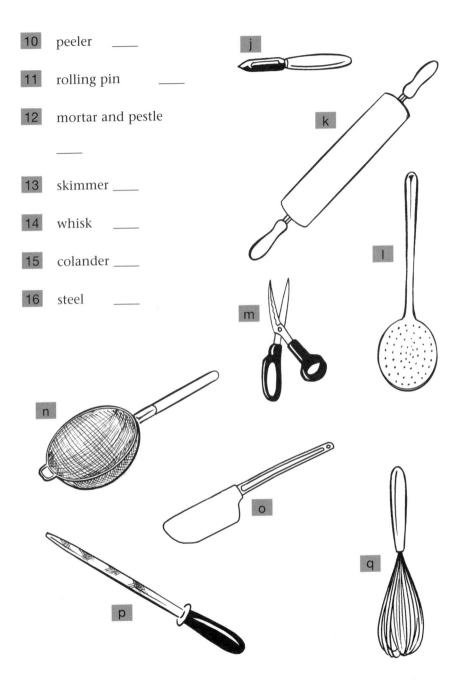

32 At work in the kitchen

Match these definitions with each of the phrasal verbs in **bold type**.

---

become	become popular	become rotten	break a promise

become   become popular   become rotten   break a promise

cause (an object) to fall to the ground   ~~continue~~   discuss again

dispose of   find information in a book   learn   not have any left

omit   reduce   require   suggest   take control   try to get

---

1   Stop wasting time and **get on with** your work!   _continue_

2   I've just been down to the store and we **are out of** flour. _____

3   If this milk isn't put in the fridge, it will **go off**. _____

4   If you're not sure of the quantity to use, **look** it **up**. _____

5   When I've prepared the sauce, you can **take over** and complete the dish. _____

6   I've explained this once already, but let's **go over** it to make sure you understand. _____

7   It looks very complicated, but you'll soon **pick** it **up**. _____

8   This machine has broken down again. We **could** really **do with** a new one. _____

9   If you continue to beat the cream, it will **turn into** butter. _____

10   Don't put that bowl there. Someone will **knock** it **over**. _____

11 You promised to cook tomorrow and you can't
    back out of it now.   _____

12 I don't think beer ice-cream will ever
    catch on, do you?   _____

13 The sauce is too sweet. You'll have to **cut down
    on** the amount of sugar you use.   _____

14 We'll have to **throw** all that yoghurt **out**.
    It's out-of-date.   _____

15 Chef wants to **drum up** business with his
    new Italian menu.   _____

16 What a disaster! You've **left out** the yeast!   _____

17 They've **put forward** plans for new kitchens.
    They certainly look good!   _____

If you're not sure of the quantity to use, look it up.

Phrasal verbs are often used in spoken English in informal situations and
less often in written English or formal situations. There are often several
possible meanings for each phrasal verb and this is often the basis of
English jokes.

33 Carriers of disease

Write the letter of each picture next to the correct word or words.

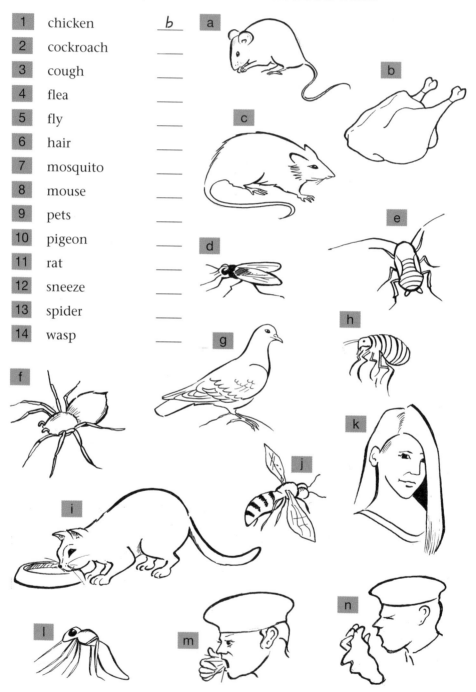

1	chicken	b
2	cockroach	___
3	cough	___
4	flea	___
5	fly	___
6	hair	___
7	mosquito	___
8	mouse	___
9	pets	___
10	pigeon	___
11	rat	___
12	sneeze	___
13	spider	___
14	wasp	___

34 Health and hygiene

A   Match the verbs on the left with a word or phrase on the right.

harbour	infection
come	diseases
dispose	separate
transmit	into contact with
spread	pain
keep	germs
relieve	of waste
contaminate	food

B   Complete each sentence with one of the combinations above. Use each combination once only.

a   Damp towels and cloths left lying in a warm place will _harbour_ _germs_ .

b   Don't spray fly-killer in the kitchen or you could _____ the _____ .

c   If you burn your hand, hold it under cold, running water to _____ the _____ .

d   If you are handling dirty linen, wash your hands regularly so that you don't _____ _____ .

e   If you _____ _____ _____ _____ animal droppings, please wash your hands immediately.

f   To _____ _____ _____ safely, place it in these plastic bags and tie them securely.

g   In the fridge please _____ raw meat and cheese _____ .

h   A kitchen should not have mice or rats because they _____ _____ .

A good way to learn vocabulary is to learn words which are often used together. These are known as collocations, e.g. *spread infection, relieve pain, contaminate food.*

35 What type of service?

A Complete the missing letters in these words.

a Silver, French, or family are examples of *t a b l e* service.

b Serving customers sitting around a bar is bar c _ _ _ _ _ _ service.

c A carvery or buffet are examples of a _ _ _ _ _ _ _ service.

d Customers use a tray and choose with s _ _ _ - service.

e A tray in hospital and meals delivered to the house are examples of in s _ _ _ service.

f Take away, drive-thrus and vending are examples of s _ _ _ _ _ p _ _ _ _ service.

B Now match the type of table service with the definition.

family	_a_	plate	____
French	____	Russian	____
gueridon	____	silver	____
mixed	____		

a All the food is served in serving dishes which are placed on the table so that the guests can help themselves.

b The food is put on the individual plates in the kitchen.

c The guests help themselves from serving dishes which are held by the waiter.

d The waiter stands at a side table and serves the food from a serving dish, using a spoon and fork.

e The waiter stands at a side table and serves the food from a serving dish using a fork and a spoon.

f The waiter carves, fillets or cooks food at a side table and then places the food on a plate.

g The main food is put on a plate in the kitchen but the vegetables are put on the table in serving dishes so that the guests can help themselves.

- **Silver service** is also known as **English service, Plate service** as **American service** and **French service** as **Butler service**.

- When serving food, it is polite for a waiter or waitress to say, **Enjoy your meal!** When the empty dishes are removed they may ask, **Did you enjoy your meal?** or **Was everything to your satisfaction?**

36 Service items

Fill in the crossword. Each answer is an item found in the dining room. Some letters have been added to help you.

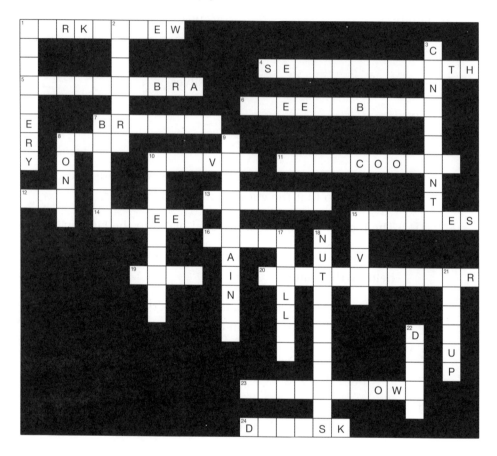

Across

1   Used to open the wine bottle.

4   It hangs over the waiter's arm. (7, 5)

5   Place this on the table. It holds several candles.

6   Cheese is served on this.

7   The team of people working in the restaurant.

8   Carry the plates on this.

10   Carry the drinks on this.

11	White wine should be placed in this to reduce the temperature. (4, 6)
12	Put water or milk in this.
13	Cigarette smokers will need this.
14	Soup is served from this.
15	The fold marks in the tablecloth.
16	Salt and pepper set.
19	Serve the toast in a toast ...
20	Used to open a bottle of beer. (6, 6)
23	The guests use this to clean their fingers. (6, 4)
24	The best quality cloth for table linen.

Down

1	A word for plates, bowls, cups, etc.
2	A word for knives, forks, spoons, etc.
3	Another word for seasoning.
7	Bread is served in a bread ...
8	Used for serving asparagus.
9	It stops the tea leaves going into the cup. (3, 8)
10	It holds necessary items and provides a work surface for the waiters.
15	A place for one person at the table.
17	Sweets can be wheeled to the table on this.
18	Used to break the shells of nuts.
21	Serve a boiled egg in this. (3, 3)
22	Place this on the plate under the biscuits.

37 A menu

Write each of these dishes in the appropriate section of the menu. The first one has been done as an example.

Leaf spinach with diced bacon

Herring and apple salad

Braised leg of lamb

Vegetable lasagne

Broccoli with hollandaise sauce

Bavarian apple strudel

Cauliflower with almonds

Mushroom stroganoff

Chef's mushroom and garlic pâté

Profiteroles with melted chocolate

Supreme of chicken sevillana

Potato croquettes

Calvados and apple brûlée

Avocado filled with prawns

Crème caramel

Roast pheasant en croûte

Entrecôte steak

Roast potatoes

Escalope of veal

Mixed seasonal salad

French onion soup

Iced cucumber soup

THE GRAPEVINE
Menu

Appetisers

Salad

Main Courses

Vegetables and Side Dishes

Leaf spinach with diced bacon

Desserts

Coffee

Appetizers may also be called **hors d'oeuvres** or **starters**. **Main courses** may be called **entrées** in more formal menus. **Desserts** are sometimes known as **sweets**.

38 Giving service

Complete the dialogues with these lines. Use each line once only.

a   Ice and lemon with the gin, sir?

b   And what would you like to drink?

c   If you like fish, I can recommend the salmon steaks. The salmon is fresh from Scotland.

d   Dry or medium white wine?

e   I'm sorry, but we're out of pineapple juice. We have orange or apple.

f   Are you ready to order, madam?

'Are you ready to order, madam?'   'I'm still looking ...'

In the restaurant

Waiter: (1) _Are you ready to order, madam?_

Guest: I'm still looking. What can you recommend?

Waiter: (2) _____

Guest: I'll have the salmon, then.

At the bar

Waiter: Yes, sir?

Guest: A gin and tonic and a glass of white wine, please.

Waiter: (3) _____

Guest: Yes, please.

Waiter: (4) _____

Guest: Dry, please.

In the snack bar

Waiter: Hello. Are you ready to order?

Guest: Yes, I think so. We'll have one cheeseburger and one hamburger.

Waiter: (5) _____

Guest: I'll have a pineapple juice and a mineral water for my girlfriend.

Waiter: (6) _____

Guest: Orange, please.

39 A breakfast tray

Write the letter of each item next to the correct word or words.

1	butter dish	_l_	**7**	saucer	____
2	coffee pot	____	**8**	small knife	____
3	cup	____	**9**	small napkin	____
4	dessert plate	____	**10**	sugar bowl	____
5	jam dish	____	**11**	teaspoon	____
6	milk jug	____	**12**	toast plate	____

40 How to be polite

Read the phrases on the left; then write them more politely. Use each phrase once only.

Actually   Could you   I'm afraid   ~~Just a moment~~   May I suggest
Please   Shall I   There's been a slight misunderstanding
Would you like   Would you like me   Would you mind

More polite

1. Wait a minute!
   Just a moment , please.

2. We haven't got any left.
   ＿＿＿＿＿＿＿＿ we haven't got any left.

3. Sit down, please.
   ＿＿＿＿＿＿＿＿ take a seat.

4. No, I'm not the head waiter.
   ＿＿＿＿＿＿＿＿ , I'm not the head waiter.

5. Do you want some water?
   ＿＿＿＿＿＿＿＿ some water?

6. Move to another table!
   ＿＿＿＿＿＿＿＿ moving to another table?

7. Confirm that tomorrow, please.
   ＿＿＿＿＿＿＿＿ confirm that tomorrow, please?

8. Do you want a taxi?
   ＿＿＿＿＿＿＿＿ to get you a taxi?

9. You've got the wrong date.
   ＿＿＿＿＿＿＿＿ about the date.

10. Try this organic wine.
    ＿＿＿＿＿＿＿＿ that you try this organic wine?

11. Do you want my help?
    ＿＿＿＿＿＿＿＿ help you?

Remember that *would you mind* is followed by *–ing*, e.g. *Would you mind waiting* here? *Would you mind signing* the bill? Try to make sentences of your own using the expressions in the box above. **See also:** Tests 2 and 3 Helping Guests.

41 Safety first

Write the letter of each item next to the correct word or words.

1	ambulance	_f_
2	bandages	___
3	cotton wool	___
4	fire alarm	___
5	fire bucket	___
6	fire escape	___
7	fire notice	___
8	first-aid box	___
9	plasters	___
10	smoke detector	___
11	sprinkler	___
12	warning sign	___

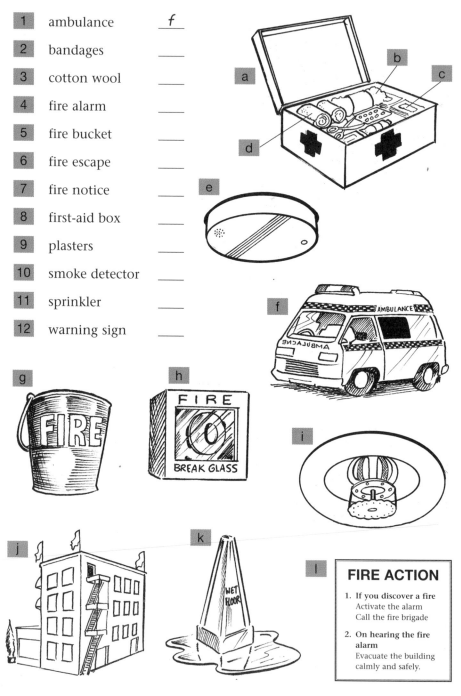

FIRE ACTION

1. **If you discover a fire**
   Activate the alarm
   Call the fire brigade

2. **On hearing the fire alarm**
   Evacuate the building calmly and safely.

42 Fire procedures

SECTION 6

This is a fire notice for hotel employees. Complete each instruction with one of these words. Use each word once only.

doors drill enter evacuate exit extinguish extinguisher lifts raise safe service smoke spread

FIRE NOTICE

1 Ask guests to check where the nearest fire _____exit_____ is located as soon as they find their room.

2 There will be a fire _____ for everyone working in the hotel every six months.

3 All fire _____ must be kept closed at all times as they will stop the _____ of a fire.

4 If you see a small fire, you should try to _____ it.

5 If it is an electrical fire, do not use a water fire _____ .

6 If it is a large fire, _____ the alarm immediately.

7 Do not use the _____ if there is a fire.

8 If there is a lot of _____ , cover your mouth and nose with a handkerchief.

9 _____ the building as quickly as possible.

10 Do not allow anyone to _____ the building.

11 Check that everyone is _____ .

12 Phone the fire _____ .

Section 6: Responsibilities **59**

43 Security measures

The word in capitals at the end of each sentence can be used to form an adjective that fits suitably in the blank space.

1 The hotel asks guests not to leave ___*valuable*___   VALUE
   pieces of jewellery in the room.

2 This area of the hotel is only for _____   AUTHORITY
   personnel.

3 Make sure that the gardeners are wearing   PROTECT
   _____ clothing when working
   with dangerous equipment.

4 The new alarm system works very well. It's easy
   to operate and _____ .   RELY

5 The receptionist called the police because there   SUSPECT
   was a _____ woman loitering at
   the rear of the hotel.

6 Computerised door locks are one of the new
   _____ measures introduced to stop   PREVENT
   thieves getting into the rooms.

7 It is _____ not to have a regular routine for
   taking cash to the bank.   ADVICE

8 Valuable items should be marked with codes
   which are only _____ under UV light.   VISION

9 Plans to evacuate the building in the case of
   an emergency must be well _____ .   ORGANIZE

10   Guests using the terrace after rain are asked to
be very _____ as it can be slippery.   CARE

11   Members of staff who prove themselves to be
_____ will be given more responsibility.   TRUST

12   Study all the alternatives available before deciding
on a _____ security system.   SUIT

Guests using the terrace after rain are asked to be very _____ .

Adjectives often end in **-able**, **-ible**, **-ful**, and **-ive**. Can you think of some more adjectives which end in these suffixes? **See also:** Test 5 At work in the front office for more word-building exercises.

44 Security risks

Match each possible situation (a–l) with the security risk (1–9) they represent. There is more than one example for some of the security risks.

1 arson   _f_

2 assault   _____

3 burglary   _____

4 fraud   _____

5 robbery   _____

6 terrorism   _____

7 theft   _____

8 undesirables   _____

9 vandalism   _____

a The beautiful porcelain vase in the lounge could be stolen.

b The manager could be attacked taking money to the bank and the money stolen.

c A customer might try to pay with a stolen credit card.

d An angry customer could become violent and hit someone.

e People sometimes break and damage items in the rooms intentionally.

f There are some people who deliberately set fire to buildings.

g You don't want drug traffickers or prostitutes using the hotel.

h The hotel could be the target of a bomb threat.

i Customers or employees may try to make false claims for damage.

j Someone could break into guest rooms and steal valuables.

k Members of staff might steal alcohol and food.

l People who have had too much to drink may begin fighting.

45 Legal words

Use the clues to fill in the missing letters in the legal words.

1	The laws which businesses must observe.	_l_ egislatio _n_
2	Responsible if someone is injured anywhere in the hotel.	_ iabl _
3	To refuse to let someone enter the bar.	_ xclud _
4	Someone who buys something.	_ urchase _
5	Someone who sells something.	_ endo _
6	An official agreement between two parties.	_ ontrac _
7	The person who owns the hotel.	_ roprieto _
8	You pay this if you are caught breaking the law.	_ in _
9	You mustn' sell alcohol to someone under the age limit. It's …	_ rohibite _
10	Official document showing permission has been given to sell alcohol.	_ icenc _
11	The person who has permission to sell alcohol.	_ icense _
12	Allow someone to enter a club.	_ dmi _
13	To enter the private areas of the hotel without permission.	_ respas _
14	Leaving dangerous chemicals where children could find them.	_ egligenc _
15	The police will do this to lawbreakers.	_ rosecut _
16	You must report serious accidents. It's …	_ ompulsor _

See also: Test 46 What do they mean?

46 What do they mean?

The following phrases are often found in official documents. Choose the best meaning for each of the phrases.

1   to comply with the law
   a) to do as the law states
   b) to change parts of the law
   c) to complain about the law

2   food unfit for human consumption
   a) food which should not be eaten
   b) food which gives energy
   c) food which is being prepared

3   must be used solely for the purpose of
   a) should not be used too often
   b) should only be used for
   c) must not be used

4   intoxicating drinks
   a) drinks which contain alcohol
   b) drinks which contain bubbles of gas
   c) drinks which contain little or no sugar

5   to be needlessly exposed to risk
   a) there are dangers in using machinery
   b) there are problems which are hidden
   c) there are dangers which could easily be removed

6   to sustain personal injury
   a) to get an insurance policy
   b) to be hurt
   c) to get promotion

7 to make available for inspection
 a) to find time to maintain the machines
 b) to arrange to clean the machine
 c) to let inspectors see what they wish

8 in the event of an accident
 a) after an accident
 b) if there is an accident
 c) to avoid accidents

9 persons frequenting the premises
 a) people cleaning the hotel
 b) people outside
 c) people using the hotel

10 a breach of contract
 a) an action which breaks a contract
 b) an added appendix to a contract
 c) an action which is included in a contract

11 to be legally obliged to
 a) you must
 b) it is allowed
 c) you shouldn't

47 Employment

Fill in the crossword. Some letters have been added to help you.

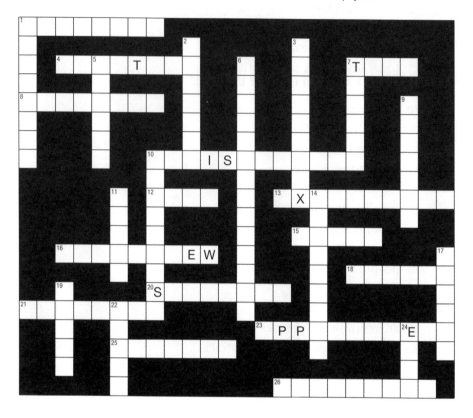

Across

1 A person who is in employment.

4 This type of job is only for a few hours a week. (4,4)

7 Extra money given by guests to say thank-you for good service.

8 If you work extra hours you get paid this.

10 People who enjoy their work have job _____ .

12 The manager appointed him to the _____ of head waiter.

13 The more jobs you do and the more years you spend working, the more of this you get.

15 Extra money that workers get from the management.

16 The meeting when you are assessed for a possible new job.

18 If you decide to leave the job, you have to _____ .

20 A hotel which is very busy in the summer will need _____ workers.

21 To get the best results from workers, the manager must _____ them.

23 When you arrange to meet and discuss a matter you make an _____ .

25 Money paid to people who have reached the official age to stop working.

26 Someone who has replied to an advertisement for a job.

Down

1 The person or company who employs you.

2 To find suitable people and employ them is to _____ .

3 A percentage of what you earn which you pay to the State. (6,3)

5 When people reach the official age to stop working they _____ .

6 People get these if they study and pass professional exams.

7 A phrasal verb which means employ. (4,2)

9 When you get a new job, the manager will _____ you to the position.

10 The housekeeper has to _____ the work of the cleaning staff.

11 People who are paid weekly or monthly receive _____ .

14 When you move up to a more senior position, you get _____ .

17 The time that you start work is the time you come _____ . (2,4)

19 A word for all the people who work in the hotel or restaurant.

22 Write a letter and _____ for the job if you are interested.

24 When you work, you _____ money.

When an employee **resigns** from a job they **give** their **notice**. This may be a written letter or given verbally and states when they intend to leave.

48 Whose job is it?

Match each task (a–n) with the correct job (1–14). The first one has been done as an example.

1	advance reservations clerk	_k_
2	banqueting manager	___
3	cashier	___
4	cellarman	___
5	chef	___
6	dispense bartender	___
7	enquiry clerk	___
8	head waiter	___
9	housekeeper	___
10	house porter	___
11	pastry cook	___
12	personnel manager	___
13	receptionist	___
14	waiter/waitress	___

a Someone has to make sure that everything in the guests' rooms is in order.

b Mika and Eri Suetake would like to discuss arrangements for their daughter's wedding reception.

c The guests' bills need to be prepared.

d Someone has to make sure there is enough wine, beer and spirits.

e The sheets and towels have to be taken upstairs.

f Four guests have just entered the restaurant.

g The waiter wants wine and beer for his tables.

h A special cake should be made for the function.

i The busy summer season is approaching and more staff are required.

j Someone should plan the cooking times for dinner.

k Someone needs to reply to this letter booking two rooms for next month.

l Someone has to welcome guests and complete the registration form.

m The guests at table eight are ready to order.

n There is a lady on the phone wanting to know if there is a room available at the weekend.

Someone has to make sure that everything in the guests' rooms is in order.

In a smaller establishment one person may have to do several jobs. In large establishments there may be several ranks from senior to junior.

49 Job advertisements

Find words or phrases in the advertisements which mean the following.

1	only for select and wealthy guests	_exclusive_
2	an applicant's list of qualifications and experience	
3	equipped	
4	minimum of	
5	looking for	
6	open for some time and known to be good	
7	chances of promotion	
8	extras to wages/salary	
9	applicants	
10	able to develop new ideas	
11	at the start	
12	salary equal to or higher than at other hotels	

Receptionists

This exclusive hotel in the heart of the city is currently seeking candidates with enthusiasm and initiative. We offer excellent benefits, good prospects and competitive pay. At least two years' experience essential.

Please call Linda Bolam
on 020 79213579

The
Pear Tree
London

HEAD CHEF

Energetic and innovative chef required initially to work with chef/proprietor and later to take over established restaurant. The kitchens are fitted out to the highest standard. We are known locally for our fish specialities. Own flat available.

Write enclosing C.V. to Pilar Alonso,
The Woodlands, Wayside Road, Oakton
MN13 9EJ
www.thewoodlands.com

50 Positive thinking

Here are some words or phrases which are used to describe hotels and their facilities. Complete the spider diagram by writing each word or phrase in the appropriate place. Some have been done for you.

appetizing	mouth-watering
beachside	nourishing
beautifully decorated	peaceful
bright	picturesque setting
central	popular family
~~cheerful~~	romantic
conveniently situated	spacious
elegant	~~tastefully furnished~~
gourmet	~~traditional~~
grand	tranquil
~~highly recommended~~	~~welcoming~~
~~home cooked~~	well-appointed
hospitable	~~well-located~~
ideally placed	well-run
modern	

This is a useful way to organize vocabulary to help you remember it. These words are all used as adjectives but you could use this system to organize nouns, verbs and adverbs as well.

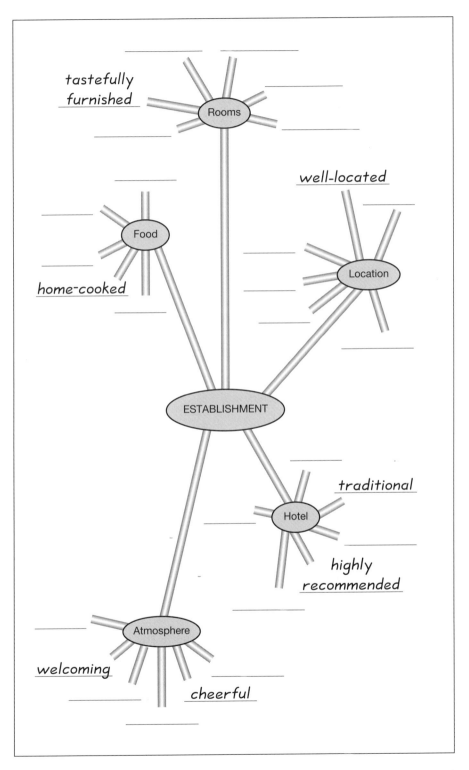

Rooms
tastefully furnished

Food
home-cooked

Location
well-located

ESTABLISHMENT

Hotel
traditional
highly recommended

Atmosphere
welcoming
cheerful

51 Marketing

Choose the word which best completes each sentence.

1 To find out about your customers, their needs and how much money they are willing to spend you can ask them to complete __questionnaire__ .
a) an enquiry form   (b) a questionnaire   c) a booking form

2 To be successful the outlet must _____ the needs of the customer.
a) satisfy   b) provide   c) decide

3 The establishment will become successful if it can gain an advantage over its _____ .
a) competitors   b) competitions   c) conquerors

4 In marketing, the establishment must consider the amount of _____ income its customers have.
a) spending   b) personal   c) disposable

5 One approach to researching the market is a SWOT analysis which looks at the strengths, weaknesses, _____ and threats.
a) opponents   b) opportunities   c) offers

6 A pricing structure which considers what customers are likely to be able to spend in the future and from that calculates what can be charged today is known as _____ pricing.
a) marginal   b) competitive   c) backward

7 The process intended to raise the profile of the establishment, persuading people to visit and return is known as _____ .
a) public relations   b) imaging   c) promotion

8 An advertising _____ will probably include different
ways of attracting new customers.
a) campaign   b) activity   c) action

9 Advertising can be done in posters, magazines, newspapers, on
radio or television or by direct mail depending on the
_____ customers.
a) objective   b) target   c) aimed

10 An establishment may decide to offer _____ to customers
who eat early in order to attract more custom.
a) discounts   b) orders   c) refunds

11 Some restaurants or hotels organise themed weekends which will
give them _____ in the local newspapers and radio.
a) publications   b) publishing   c) publicity

12 The staff are very important in creating a good _____ for
the establishment.
a) sign   b) image   c) reflection

13 Goods such as pens, T-shirts and matchboxes which help promote
the establishment are known as _____ .
a) merchandising   b) demonstrating   c) side-lining

14 All establishments rely on satisfied customers telling their friends
and colleagues by _____ .
a) putting words in their mouth   b) word of mouth
c) taking their word for it

15 The process of building a good reputation in the eyes of the
customers, employees and investors is known as _____ .
a) good relations   b) public relations   c) public confidence

52 Computer systems

Rearrange the letters to form the correct words.

1 Information can be typed into the computer
using a ___*keyboard*___ .   RYEKDBOA

2 Pictures, photographs and diagrams can be
entered using a _____ .   NANSCER

3 People using the computer can see the
information on a _____ .   ENESCR

4 A _____ can be used for writing
letters, memos and reports as well as
producing menus.   WRDO PRSORCESO

5 It's sometimes necessary to have computer
information on paper in the form of
a _____ .   PRTOUINT

6 There is a wide range of _____
available to the hospitality industry,
e.g. reservations, food and beverage
management.   APATIONPLSIC

7 Many large hotel groups use a _____
reservations system which links different
establishments directly.   CERALNT

8 Customers who have computers may choose
to make reservations on the _____ .   ITERNTEN

9 These systems often have a direct
connection or _____ to airlines
or travel agents to allow direct reservations.   INFACETER

10 The traditional cash register has been
replaced by an electronic _____ .   PNTOI FO EASL

11 This includes _____ , where the
waiter simply presses a key for the
required dish or drink.   PCIRE LKOO PU

12 Information can also be entered by
using a _____ terminal.   TCHUO SCNREE

13 Computers used in bars to measure exact
amounts of spirits are called _____ .   OPCTIS

14 In a large hotel several computers will
be joined together or _____ .   NEEDWORTK

15 At the end of a shift, members of staff
have to _____ .   OGL FOF

16 The food and beverage management
system will include a _____
of all the recipes used in the establishment.   DABSTAAE

17 Each ingredient has its own _____ .   CDEO

18 Some establishments may also
have add-on _____ to allow
nutritional analysis.   MOLESDU

19 Linen control can be greatly improved with
an identification system which uses labels
with _____ which can be quickly
read on a scanner.   RBA DESCO

20 Many hotels are trying to increase security
by using a _____ system which
records every time a lock is opened and
by whom.   YEK DARC

53 At work in the office

Complete the sentences with one of these prepositions. Some of the prepositions are used more than once.

about	for	from	in	of	on	to	with

1 Could you take care __*of*__ the seating arrangements for the conference?

2 Mrs Brown has complained _____ the manager _____ the food.

3 The number of staff depends _____ the season.

4 Something seems to have happened _____ this plant. It's dead!

5 We still haven't heard _____ those clients who requested flowers.

6 All employees are expected to be loyal _____ the company.

7 I'm relying _____ you to sort out this problem peacefully.

8 I'll think _____ how to promote your idea of a Japanese night, and we'll discuss it later.

9 We should provide our cleaners _____ new uniforms.

10 I'm glad you reminded me _____ the meeting. I'd forgotten!

11 Any telephone costs will be added _____ the bill.

12 Everyone is responsible _____ maintaining high standards in the establishment.

13 The manager is very pleased _____ this month's sales figures.

14 Our restaurant is famous _____ its fish dishes.

15 It's been so cold that there's been no demand _____ soft drinks.

16 They insisted _____ paying for the reception in cash.

17 Don't leave things lying around or it could result _____ an accident.

They insisted _____ paying for the reception in cash.

Try to learn appropriate prepositions together with new vocabulary, e.g. *take care of*, *depend on*, and *famous for*. A good dictionary will help you. **See also:** Test 13 Giving directions.

54 Office items

Write the letter of each item next to the correct word or words.

1	adhesive tape	_d_
2	calculator	___
3	desk diary	___
4	diskette	___
5	foldback clip	___
6	hole punch	___
7	notepad	___
8	paper clips	___
9	planner	___
10	ring binder	___
11	ruler	___
12	stapler	___
13	suspension file	___
14	trays	___
15	window envelope	___

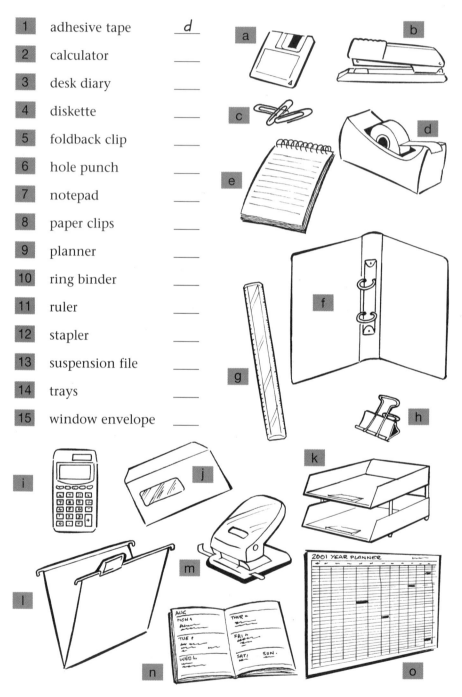

55 Handling stock

The bin card is one type of record used in stores control. There should be a bin card for each item held in stock.

A Fill in the bin card headings. Choose from the following:

Balance	Date	In	Item	Maximum	Minimum	Price
Quantity	~~Reference~~	Suppliers	Type	Unit		

| _____ : Sherry | _____ : 75 cl bottle |
| _____ : Amontillado | _____ : £3.22 |

_____	_Reference_	_____	**Out**	_____
1st Oct	JB	24		24
2nd Oct	BP		6	18
4th Oct	JB		3	15
6th Oct	JB	24		39
7th Oct	BP		10	29
_____				
_____				
_____				

_____ stock: 48   _____ stock: 8

Re-order point: 24   _____ : Classic Wine Importers Ltd

Re-order _____ : 24

B Update the card with the following information.

a On 8th October 8 bottles were issued by John Bridges.

b On 12th October 24 bottles were received from the suppliers by John Bridges.

c Barbara Palm took 10 bottles on 13th October.

In addition to **bin cards**, a **stores ledger** is used. The balance on the bin card should be the same as the balance on the stores ledger sheet.

56 Business documentation

Use the clues to fill in the missing letters. The first one has been done as an example.

1. When goods are required, an _____ is sent to an external supplier.

   ord *e* *r*

2. When the goods are delivered, this list of goods is often enclosed.

   de _ _ _ _ _ _ n _ _ _

3. After delivery, the supplier provides a list of the total goods sent, giving quantity and price.

   in _ _ _ _ _

4. If you pay within seven days, you can often get a ...

   c _ _ _ di _ _ _ _ _ _

5. If you buy regularly from the local baker he may allow you a ...

   tr _ _ _ di _ _ _ _ _ _

6. At the end of the month most suppliers send out this list of everything bought and all money paid.

   st _ _ _ _ _ _ _

7. If goods have to be returned to the supplier, he will send this to adjust the amount of money due.

   c _ _ _ _ _ n _ _ _

8. This will be sent if a customer doesn't pay his account.

   r _ _ _ _ der

9. The official document from a government department allowing the establishment to trade.

   l _ _ _ _ ce

All items made to be bought and sold are known as **goods. Suppliers** are people, companies and organisations that provide goods.

57 Accountancy terms

Complete the sentences with one of these words. Use each phrase once only.

cash float	credit	credit customer accounts	creditors	debit
debtors	~~double entry~~	payroll	petty cash book	posted
	purchase ledger	visitors' paid-outs		

1 Most companies use a system of accounting known as
double entry .

2 This divides the page into two columns which are called
_____ and _____ .

3 Suppliers who have not yet received payment for goods which
they have already delivered are _____ .

4 Customers who have not yet paid their bills are _____ .

5 The accounts of suppliers to the hotel are kept in the
_____ .

6 The accounts of customers are known as _____ .

7 When figures are moved from one account to another they are
_____ .

8 All the information needed to pay staff wages and salaries is on
the _____ .

9 Small amounts of cash which are paid out are recorded in the
_____ .

10 Small items of cash which are paid out on behalf of a guest are
called _____ .

11 At the start of each day the bar and restaurant staff are given a
fixed amount of cash which is called a _____ .

58 Final accounts

Match each word (1–13) with its definition (a–m). The first one has been done as an example.

1	profit and loss account	_k_	8	bad debts	___
2	trading account	___	9	depreciation	___
3	balance sheet	___	10	budget	___
4	fixed assets	___	11	overheads	___
5	current assets	___	12	stock	___
6	long-term liabilities	___	13	break-even point	___
7	current liabilities	___			

a   includes cash in the safe and in the bank

b   bills which will never be paid

c   when sales equal costs – no profit or loss

d   regular expenses including rent, telephone, gas, advertising

e   shows the gross profit at the end of the year

f   furniture, kitchen equipment, crockery, etc.

g   food, liquor, and tobacco still in store

h   a statement at the end of the year showing how the company is financed

i   borrowed money which will be paid back over a long period of time

j   money which will be paid to suppliers soon

k   shows the net profit after electricity, rent, stationery, etc. has been deducted

l   reduction in value of machines and furniture over several years

m   planned financial figures for the future

59 Nationalities and currencies

A Complete the table.

Country	People	Language	Currency	
	Australians		dollar	(AUD)
Canada		English/French		(CAD)
China			yuan renminbi	(CNY)
Germany		German		
		Bahasa	rupiah	(IDR)
	Japanese	Japanese		(JPY)
	Norwegians	Norwegian		(NOK)
Poland		Polish		(PLZ)
		Russian	rouble	(RUR)
Switzerland		German/French/Italian/ Rheto-Romansch		(CHf)
United Kingdom	British	English	pound	(GBP)
United States of America	Americans			(USD)

B Now use the words from the table to complete the sentences.

a For France and Germany, what is the exchange rate for American dollars into _____ ?

b You're from Poland! I'm afraid I don't speak _____ .

c These guests are from China but I can't speak _____ .

d The guests in room 147 are _____ , from Tokyo.

e How many _____ will I get for 500 euro in Norway?

f Our guests from the _____ want to pay in their own currency: US dollars.

g Can we accept _____ from our Russian guests?

h Can you tell me the rate of the Swiss _____ today?

60 Facts and figures

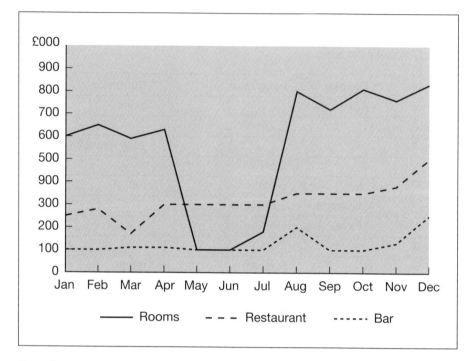

Complete the missing words in the presentation below. Use each word once only.

at   back   ~~borrow~~   decrease   dramatic   finance   fluctuated
improved   interest   loan   off   remained   rise   rose   slowly
small   steady   steeply   to   with

Last year was a very difficult year for the hotel. Major improvements were carried out during the summer. We had to (1) ___*borrow*___ money from the bank to (2) _____ this work. We are now dependent on increased sales to pay the monthly (3) _____ on this (4) _____ , which we hope to be able to pay (5) _____ in five years.

From the graph you can see that the most (6) _____ sales figures were from the income from rooms. We began building work in May and this had an enormous effect on sales which fell (7) _____ (8) _____ £100,000 and (9) _____ at that level during June. In July we reopened with a massive advertising campaign and saw sales (10) _____ rapidly to reach £800,000 by the end of August. For the rest of the year sales (11) _____ slightly.

As far as the restaurant is concerned, we can see that at the beginning of the year turnover stood (12) _____ £250,000. Over the next two months sales increased (13) _____ , but there was a (14) _____ of £100,000 in March. Things (15) _____ again in April and then levelled (16) _____ at £300,000. In August, as the number of hotel guests increased, we began to see a rise in restaurant sales which then remained (17) _____ over the following three months. In December, sales (18) _____ steeply with corporate functions leading up to Christmas.

Bar sales remained fairly constant throughout the year although there was a (19) _____ increase in August. This was probably due to local people viewing the completed renovations. Of course there was a significant rise in December in line (20) _____ the restaurant sales.

> The verb **rise** does not take an object, e.g. *the sun rises, prices rose.* However, the verb **raise** takes an object, e.g. *they are raising prices, the government raised taxes.* **Rise** is also used as a noun, e.g. *there was a rise in sales.*

British English and American English

British English	American English
accommodation	accommodations
aubergine	egg plant
barman	bartender
bill (for food)	check
biscuit	cookie
cheque	check
colour	color
courgette	zucchini
cupboard, wardrobe	closet
curtains	drapes
fill in a form	fill out a form
fridge	icebox
handbag	purse
holiday	vacation
iron	press
labour	labor
lager	beer
left luggage	baggage room
licence	license
lift	elevator
main course	entrée
note (paper money)	bill
page boy	bell boy, bell hop, page
post	mail
provisional	unconfirmed
pub	saloon/bar
reception	front desk/front office
receptionist	clerk, desk clerk
rubbish	garbage/trash
shop	store
spirit	liquor
starter	appetiser
sunglasses	shades
tap	faucet
taxi	cab
toilet	bathroom, restroom, washroom
traveller's cheques	travelers checks
turnover	revenue
venue	locale
waiter	waiter/food server
wallet	billfold
washbasin	sink

Answers

Section 1: The front office

Test 1

1 corridor	9 terrace
2 kiosk	10 lounge
3 balcony	11 stairs
4 laundry	12 lift
5 lobby	13 cloakroom
6 cocktail bar	14 kitchen
7 left luggage	15 banqueting room
8 cellar	

Test 2

1 a 2 f 3 g 4 d 5 c 6 e 7 b 8 h

Test 3

1 e 2 l 3 g 4 b 5 j 6 a 7 k 8 h 9 f
10 i 11 d 12 c

Test 4

1 b 2 b 3 c 4 a 5 c 6 a 7 c 8 c 9 a
10 b 11 d 12 d

Test 5

1 reservation
2 arrangements
3 confirmation
4 requirements
5 availability
6 satisfaction
7 cancellation
8 expectations
9 allocation
10 correspondence
11 entries
12 vacancies
13 entertainment
14 appreciation

Test 6

1 Letter of reservation: e, c, g, h, b, a
2 Letter of confirmation: k, f, i, d, j

Test 7

1 check out	7 calculate
2 incur	8 settle
3 sign for	9 return
4 issue	10 dispute
5 itemize	11 liaise
6 vacate	12 overcharge

Test 8

1 credit card
2 exchange rate
3 foreign currency
4 sales voucher
5 travel agent's voucher
6 service charge
7 travellers cheques
8 property management
9 ledger account
10 commission rate
11 bank notes

Test 9

1 a 2 d 3 h 4 i 5 c 6 f 7 m 8 g 9 k
10 o 11 j 12 b 13 l 14 n 15 e

Section 2: Hotel services

Test 10

Room service 3
Tariffs 12
Telephone 8
Entertainment 11
Minibar 9
Shoe-cleaning service 5
Transport 2
Wake-up calls 7
Laundry 1
Garaging 10
Medical help 4
Hairdressing and Beauty 6

Test 11

A American plan – bed, breakfast,
   lunch and dinner
   Demi-pension – bed, breakfast and
   lunch or dinner
   European plan – bed only
   Continental plan – bed and
   breakfast
B a) twin b) double c) single
   d) double en suite e) adjoining

Test 12

1	escorted	8	excursions
2	attractions	9	itinerary
3	ruins	10	souvenirs
4	galleries	11	cruise
5	museums	12	events
6	countryside	13	displayed
7	scenery	14	festivals

Test 13
1 at/before
2 opposite
3 past
4 beside/next to
5 into, on
6 across
7 on
8 on/ahead
9 along/down/up, until/till
10 on, after

Test 14
Across
3 multimedia projector
7 whiteboard
8 folding tables
10 monitor
12 theatre style
13 microphone

Down
1 classroom style
2 stacking chairs
4 overhead projector
5 refreshments
6 lobbyboard
9 flipchart
11 screen

Test 15
1 venue
2 estimated attendance
3 provisional
4 duration
5 annual
6 conference package
7 function sheet
8 finalize
9 postpone
10 delegates
11 speakers
12 seating capacity
13 square metres
14 plenary

15 syndicate
16 hospitality room
17 conference programme
18 opening ceremonies

Test 16
1 k 2 g 3 e 4 f 5 d 6 m 7 h 8 l 9 c
10 a 11 n 12 i 13 b 14 j

Test 17
1 May I ask
2 One moment
3 How can I
4 Can you tell me
5 I'm sorry to
6 I'm terribly sorry
7 Could you
8 I must apologise
9 assure
10 of course
11 deeply regret
12 if you would accept
13 at our expense
14 bringing this incident
15 right

Section 3: Housekeeping

Test 18
1 c 2 a 3 d 4 c 5 b 6 a 7 d 8 a 9 b
10 c

Test 19
1 a 2 c 3 f 4 g 5 k 6 i 7 m 8 t 9 w
10 v 11 l 12 q 13 e 14 s 15 p 16 o
17 u 18 j 19 b 20 d 21 r 22 x 23 n
24 h

Test 20
1 d 2 h 3 e 4 m 5 p 6 l 7 k 8 q
9 c 10 f 11 j 12 a 13 n 14 b 15 g
16 i 17 o

Test 21

1	sweep	8	soak
2	polish	9	dry-clean
3	scrub	10	vacuum
4	wet mop	11	strip
5	damp wipe	12	replenish
6	launder	13	dispose of
7	rinse	14	deep clean

Test 22

1	tarnish	9	bleach
2	fingerprints	10	stain
3	slippery	11	salvage
4	splash	12	rust
5	odours	13	solvents
6	abrasive	14	soilage
7	labour-saving	15	chamois
8	limescale		

Test 23

1	ventilation	8	insulated
2	humidity	9	tank
3	grill	10	pipes
4	extractor	11	drains
5	filters	12	sewer
6	radiator	13	U-bend
7	thermostat		

Test 24

1	appliances	6	kilowatt hours
2	flex	7	current
3	plug	8	overloaded
4	socket	9	electrician
5	fuse	10	wiring

Section 4: Food and drink

Test 25

1 b 2 l 3 c 4 j 5 d 6 n 7 a 8 g 9 k
10 f 11 i 12 e 13 o 14 m 15 h

Test 26

1 k 2 d 3 a 4 f 5 q 6 m 7 h 8 n
9 g 10 r 11 p 12 b 13 e 14 s 15 l
16 c 17 o 18 j 19 i

Test 27

1	dairy products	11	fish
2	nuts	12	beverages
3	pulses	13	wine
4	herbs	14	game
5	spices	15	soups
6	meat	16	cheeses
7	dried fruit	17	seafood
8	pastry	18	cakes
9	icing	19	sauces
10	pasta	20	cereals

Test 28

1	bitter	9	greasy
2	hot	10	dry
3	rich	11	delicious
4	sweet	12	burnt
5	spicy	13	salty
6	bland	14	tender
7	sour	15	stale
8	savoury	16	rancid

Test 29

1	smoking
2	canning
3	drying
4	chemicals
5	vacuum-packing
6	gas storage
7	freezing
8	salting
9	radiation
10	sugaring

Test 30

1 f 2 n 3 g 4 m 5 b 6 c 7 l 8 j 9 k
10 e 11 i 12 a 13 d 14 h

Test 31

1 h 2 m 3 d 4 c 5 g 6 f 7 e 8 o
9 a 10 j 11 k 12 i 13 l 14 q 15 b
16 p 17 n

Test 32

1	continue
2	not have any left
3	become rotten
4	find information in a book
5	take control
6	discuss again
7	learn
8	require
9	become
10	cause an object to fall to the ground
11	break a promise
12	become popular
13	reduce
14	dispose of
15	try to get
16	omit
17	suggest

Test 33
1 b 2 e 3 m 4 h 5 d 6 k 7 l 8 a 9 i
10 g 11 c 12 n 13 f 14 j

Test 34
A harbour germs
   come into contact with
   dispose of waste
   transmit diseases
   spread infection
   keep separate
   relieve pain
   contaminate food
B a) harbour germs
   b) contaminate food
   c) relieve pain
   d) spread infection
   e) come into contact with
   f) dispose of waste
   g) keep separate
   h) transmit diseases

Section 5: Food service

Test 35
A a table
   b bar counter
   c assisted
   d self
   e in situ
   f single point

B family a
   French c
   gueridon f
   mixed g
   plate b
   Russian e
   silver d

Test 36
Across
1 corkscrew
4 service cloth
5 candelabra
6 cheeseboard
7 brigade
8 tray
10 salver
11 wine cooler
12 jug
13 ashtray
14 tureen
15 creases
16 cruet
19 rack
20 bottle opener
23 finger bowl
24 damask

Down
1 crockery
2 cutlery
3 condiments
7 basket
8 tongs
9 tea-strainer
10 sideboard
15 cover
17 trolley
18 nutcrackers
21 egg cup
22 doily

Test 37
Appetisers
Chef's mushroom and garlic pâté
French onion soup
Avocado filled with prawns
Iced cucumber soup

Salads
Herring and apple salad
Mixed seasonal salad

Main courses
Braised leg of lamb
Supreme of chicken sevillana
Entrecôte steak
Escalope of veal
Roast pheasant en croûte
Vegetable lasagne
Mushroom stroganoff

Vegetables and Side Dishes
Leaf spinach with diced bacon
Broccoli with hollandaise sauce
Cauliflower with almonds
Potato croquettes
Roast potatoes

Desserts
Bavarian apple strudel
Profiteroles with melted chocolate
Crème caramel
Calvados and apple brûlée

Test 38
1 f 2 c 3 a 4 d 5 b 6 e

Test 39
1 l 2 a 3 d 4 h 5 g 6 b 7 e 8 i 9 j
10 c 11 f 12 k

Test 40
1 Just a moment
2 I'm afraid
3 Please
4 Actually
5 Would you like
6 Would you mind
7 Could you
8 Would you like me
9 There's been a slight
   misunderstanding
10 May I suggest
11 Shall I

Section 6: Responsibilities

Test 41
1 f 2 d 3 b 4 h 5 g 6 j 7 l 8 a 9 c
10 e 11 i 12 k

Test 42
1 exit	7 lifts
2 drill	8 smoke
3 doors, spread	9 Evacuate
4 extinguish	10 enter
5 extinguisher	11 safe
6 raise	12 service

Test 43
1 valuable	7 advisable
2 authorized	8 visible
3 protective	9 well organized
4 reliable	10 careful
5 suspicious	11 trustworthy
6 preventive	12 suitable

Test 44
arson f
assault b, d, l
burglary a, j
fraud c, i
robbery b
terrorism h
theft a, k
undesirables g
vandalism e

Test 45
1 legislation	9 prohibited
2 liable	10 licence
3 exclude	11 licensee
4 purchaser	12 admit
5 vendor	13 trespass
6 contract	14 negligence
7 proprietor	15 prosecute
8 fine	16 compulsory

Test 46
1 a 2 a 3 b 4 a 5 c 6 b 7 c 8 b 9 c
10 a 11 a

Section 7: Management

Test 47
Across		Down	
1	employee	1	employer
4	part-time	2	recruit
7	tips	3	income tax
8	overtime	5	retire
10	satisfaction	6	qualifications
12	post	7	take on
13	experience	9	appoint
15	bonus	10	supervise
16	interview	11	wages
18	resign	14	promotion
20	seasonal	17	on duty
21	motivate	19	staff
23	appointment	22	apply
25	pension	24	earn
26	applicant		

Test 48
1 k 2 b 3 c 4 d 5 j 6 g 7 n 8 f 9 a
10 e 11 h 12 i 13 l 14 m

Test 49
1 exclusive
2 C.V.
3 fitted out
4 at least
5 seeking
6 established
7 prospects
8 benefits
9 candidates
10 innovative
11 initially
12 competitive pay

Test 50
Rooms:
beautifully decorated
bright
elegant
spacious
tastefully furnished
well-appointed

Location:
beachside
central
conveniently situated
ideally placed
picturesque setting
well-located

Food:
appetizing
nourishing
gourmet
home-cooked
mouth-watering

Hotel:
grand
highly recommended
popular family
traditional
well-run
modern

Atmosphere:
cheerful
hospitable
peaceful
romantic
tranquil
welcoming

Test 51

1 b 2 a 3 a 4 c 5 b 6 c 7 c 8 a 9 b
10 a 11 c 12 b 13 a 14 b 15 b

Test 52

1 keyboard
2 scanner
3 screen
4 word processor
5 printout
6 applications
7 central
8 internet
9 interface
10 point of sale
11 price look up
12 touch screen
13 optics
14 networked
15 log off

16 database
17 code
18 modules
19 bar codes
20 key card

Section 8: Financial affairs

Test 53

1	of	10	about
2	to, about	11	to
3	on	12	for
4	to	13	with
5	from	14	for
6	to	15	for
7	on	16	on
8	about	17	in
9	with		

Test 54

1 d 2 i 3 n 4 a 5 h 6 m 7 e 8 c
9 o 10 f 11 g 12 b 13 l 14 k 15 j

Test 55

Item: Sherry   **Unit:** 75 cl bottle
Type: Amontillado **Price:** £3.22

Date	Reference	In	Out	Balance
1st Oct	JB	24		24
2nd Oct	BP		6	18
4th Oct	JB		3	15
6th Oct	JB	24		39
7th Oct	BP		10	29
8th Oct	**JB**		8	21
12th Oct	**JB**	24		45
13th Oct	**BP**		10	35

Maximum stock: 48
Re-order point: 24
Re-order **quantity:** 24
Minimum stock: 8
Suppliers: Classic Wine Importers Ltd

Test 56

1	order	6	statement
2	delivery note	7	credit note
3	invoice	8	reminder
4	cash discount	9	licence
5	trade discount		

Test 57

1 double entry
2 debit, credit
3 creditors
4 debtors
5 purchase ledger
6 credit customer accounts
7 posted
8 payroll
9 petty cash book
10 visitors' paid-outs
11 cash float

Test 58

1 k 2 e 3 h 4 f 5 a 6 i 7 j 8 b 9 l
10 m 11 d 12 g 13 c

Test 59

1 See table below:
2 1 euros
   2 Polish
   3 Chinese
   4 Japanese
   5 kroner
   6 United States of America/USA
   7 roubles
   8 franc

Test 60

1 borrow
2 finance
3 interest
4 loan
5 back
6 dramatic
7 steeply
8 to
9 remained
10 rise
11 fluctuated
12 at
13 slowly
14 decrease
15 improved
16 off
17 steady
18 rose
19 small
20 with

Country	People	Language	Currency
Australia	Australians	English	dollar (AUD)
Canada	Canadians	English/French	dollar (CAD)
China	Chinese	Chinese	yuan renminbi (CNY)
Germany	Germans	German	euro
Indonesia	Indonesians	Bahasa	rupiah (IDR)
Japan	Japanese	Japanese	yen (JPY)
Norway	Norwegians	Norwegian	kroner (NOK)
Poland	Polish	Polish	zloty (PLZ)
Russia	Russians	Russian	rouble (RUR)
Switzerland	Swiss	German/French/Italian/ Rheto-Romansch	franc (CHf)
United Kingdom	British	English	pound (GBP)
United States of America	Americans	English	dollar (USD)

Word list

The numbers after the entries are the tests in which they appear.

A

about 53
abrasive 22
accept 17
across 13
actually 40
adhesive tape 54
adjoining room 11
admit 45
advance reservations clerk 48
advertising campaign 51
advisable 43
after 13
ahead 13
allocation 5
almond 27
along 13
ambulance 41
American plan 11
Americans 59
american service 35
annual 15
apologise 17
appetizers 37
appetizing 50
appliance 24
applicant 47
application 52
apply 47
appoint 47
appointment 47
appreciation 5
arrangement 5
arrivals 4
arson 44
artichoke 26
ashtray 16, 36
asparagus 26
assault 44
assisted service 35
assure 17
at 13
at least 49
atmosphere 50
attraction 12
aubergine 26

Australia 59
Australians 59
authorized 43
availability 5
available for inspection 46
avocado 25

B

back out of 32
backward pricing 51
bacteria 29
bad debts 58
Bahasa 59
bake 30
balance 55
balance sheet 58
balcony 1
bandage 41
banister 19
bank note 8
banqueting manager 48
banqueting room 1
bar code 52
bar counter service 35
barley 27
basil 27
basket 36
baste 30
bath 20
bath mat 20
be out of 38
beachside 50
Bearnaise sauce 27
beautifully decorated 50
béchamel sauce 27
bedside cabinet 19
bedspread 19
beef 27
before 13
benefits 49
beside 13
Best wishes 6
beverage 27
bin card 55
binoculars 9
bitter 28
blackcurrant 25